thoughts

ia

Scarlet
Geranium

confidence

Purple
Hyacinth

Water Lily

love

ld

Peony

warmth

agreement

Dahlia

erry
n

affection

Sweet Basil

Gloxinia

Magnolia

oil

gallantry

Flowering
Almond

Phlox

Watering Wilted Flowers

A Healing Guide
for Women

Written by Ginny Goff Green • Illustrated by Deborah Keyser Dion

RUNNING PRESS
PHILADELPHIA · LONDON

Cover

Black-eyed Susan, *justice*

Text © 1998 by Virginia G. Green • Illustrations © 1998 by Deborah Dion
All rights reserved under the Pan-American
and International Copyright Conventions

Printed in China

9   8   7   6   5   4   3   2   1
Digit on the right indicates the number of this printing

Library of Congress Cataloging-in-Publication Number 97-66825

ISBN 0-7624-0234-2

Designed by Maria Taffera Lewis
Edited by Mary McGuire Ruggiero

This book may be ordered by mail from the publisher. Please include $2.50 for
postage and handling. *But try your bookstore first!*

Running Press Book Publishers
125 South Twenty-second Street
Philadelphia, Pennsylvania 19103-4399

/

Dedication

To Les and Alan

"Gloire de Dijon" Rose, *messenger of love*

Acknowledgments

I WOULD LIKE TO THANK MY FAMILY for "being there" when I wasn't sure exactly where they were or how things would go for me. I thank my mother, Elaine Benson Kaufman, for giving me a book which, though totally unrelated to this work, gave me the idea for it. She was also helpful with the manuscript, as was Renée Goff. I thank my father, Warren Goff; my siblings, Bill, Neal, and Kimberly; and my stepchildren, John and Todd Green and Jennifer Miller, for their frequent contact, their constancy, and their care.

Inspiration and ideas for parts of the text came from Norman Cousins's book *Anatomy of an Illness*, the "Johns Hopkins Medical Health Letter," Linus Pauling, Burton Lane, Jennifer Miller, Miriam Simon, and Don Henley.

My thanks also go to Alan Dion and, of course, to Debby Keyser Dion for her talent and craftsmanship and visual sense and humor.

But most of all, I want to thank my husband. He is inspirational in almost everything he does. This book would not have been without him. He has seen me through our years together with grace and support and love of great dimension.   —GGG

.   .   .

I AM MOST GRATEFUL to Ginny Green for her wonderful idea, insightful manuscript, and longstanding friendship—they made this book happen. I thank Jacqi Roberts, John F. Klaiber, Tom Shea, Marthe Roberts Shea, Carolyn Remigio; and the Victorians, for popularizing the language of flowers.

I would also like to thank my husband, Alan; my daughters, Joanna and Samantha, for their love and encouragement; my mother, Evelyn Keyser Borowsky; my stepfather, Milton Borowsky; my father, Gerson Keyser, whose memory lives on to inspire me; and Toby Schmidt Schachman for her help in getting our first work published.

I also wish to acknowledge every woman who has been diagnosed with a serious illness. You provided me the strength to work the many long hours needed to complete this book. May you live to see the day when there is a cure for that which threatens your life.   —DKD

Contents

Introduction

RECOVERING FROM CRANIAL SURGERY, I was lying in bed, looking at vases filled with daisies and irises and snapdragons, and thinking about what I was going through. I was also thinking about the fact that I would need brain surgery soon again and that even when I was totally recovered from that, I would have to contend with the lupus that continues to do its dirty-work in my brain and central nervous system. In a situation like that, you have to have a sense of humor. You also have to be creative.

The telephone rang and it was Debby Dion. She and I were best friends in junior high school. Debby's parents were both artists and she was clearly going to be one, too. At that time I thought I might become an artist—or maybe a writer.

We talked about how I was doing, realizing that only six months earlier a similar phone call became a conversation about her surgery. The irony was that I had called Debby to tell her about my brain masses (what are friends for), and her news was that she had Stage 1 breast cancer and had just had a double mastectomy and the beginnings of reconstructive surgery.

Debby and I realized that the world is full of people trying to cope with their own medical crises. Our response was to write this book.

Our thought is that *Watering Wilted Flowers* could be an alternative to buying flowers for someone who is having medical problems. That's why we filled it with flowers. Through marvelous research on Debby's part, she was able to link the meanings of the flowers to my messages. And the messages and the illustrations will last substantially longer than cut flowers. We hope that they will stay with you, and that you will renew yourself with the book whenever you're feeling a little low.

Some of our pages suggest ways to deal with whatever you are going through. Some of these suggestions might even seem like medical or legal advice. Clearly, we are not doctors or lawyers. We would appreciate it if you would regard suggestions in this book as ideas that helped Debby and me through some tough times, ideas that may help you or at least show you a direction from which to seek your own answers. If you need legal or medical advice, please talk to a licensed professional.

We believe in watering wilted flowers. Doing so brings them to their full potential.

And we hope our book brings you back to yours, providing strength and happiness and well-being in a way that other things cannot.

One

Accepting Your Diagnosis

Daffodil, *regard*

Yours is not
the worst diagnosis

If you have rheumatoid arthritis and
find out you have a brain tumor,
it is not time to despair.

Many people have it worse.

Buy a plaid flower pot.
Plant pansies.

Be thankful for your eye sight.
Be thankful for your friends.

Pansy, *thoughts*

Petunia, *never despair*

Given the choice between happy and sad, choose happy

It's the obvious choice.
It's a choice you will enjoy.

Sing "Zippety Doo Dah."
Listen to a bluebird chirp.

Lay your hand
on a purring kitten.

Face the sun and be vibrant.

Given the choice between brave and frightened, choose brave

It's the right choice.
It's a heartening choice.

Listen to a recording of
"You're a Grand Old Flag."

Pin a medal on your blouse.

Face the sun and reflect its strength.

Gladiolus, *strength of character*

Water yourself

You are like a flower.

Water cleanses
your cells
and passes impurities
out of your system.

Drink in the nectar.

Water makes you
blossom
like a lily.

Water Lily, *purity of heart*

Red Rose, *love*; Nasturtium, *patriotism*

(Rose hips and Nasturtium leaves, sources of vitamin C)

Saturate your cells
with vitamin C

Flowers need sunlight.
Humans need vitamins.

Many medicines use up your vitamin C.
And vitamin C helps you heal.

Shower your cells with fresh orange juice.
Or cran-raspberry juice, or
pomegranate juice, if you prefer.

Your stem will be strong. Your blossoms will thrive.

Pamper yourself
with knowledge

Become an expert on your condition.

Learn about your options.

When you do,
you and your doctor can become
partners in your treatment
and in your recovery.

Sweet Cherry Blossom, *good education*

Forget-me-not, *true love*

Keep a journal

Buy a blank journal
with a Tiffany stained glass cover.
Or write on whatever's at hand.

Each day, write about how you feel.
Write the details.
Keep a list of questions.

Your notes will remind you of what to say
when the doctor asks how you've been.

When you are under a lot of stress,
it's easy to forget.
When the doctor gives you information,
write it in your book.

Your notes will make it easier for you
and your doctor
to understand what's going on in your body.

Strawberry Blossom, *foresight*

Clarify your medical choices

Only you know how you feel
about life-sustaining equipment.

Your family and doctor need to know.

*Call the local Bar Association or
Medical Society.
Ask for the format of a living will.*

If you agree with what it says,
sign and date it.

Send copies
to those who would make decisions for you
if you were unable to.
Have your doctor
put it in your chart.

Then forget it.

Get to know
your medical coverage

Insurance is like a blanket—
not very interesting,
but it comes in handy when you need it.

The momentary discomfort of the dry words
gradually turns
to the comfort of understanding.

Know the details of each stem and leaf
of your plan.
Whether perfect or flawed, you stand to benefit.

Now is the time.

*Lie in the ivy of
what you know.*

Scarlet Geranium, *comforting*

China Aster, *variety*

Buy some hats and a wig

If your condition will result in hair loss,
buy a hat and a wig.

Try a flowered cotton squishy hat and
turn the brim every which way.
Slip on a denim pancake hat;
bend the brim a little.
Tilt a beret over your left eyebrow.

Go wig shopping with your hairdresser.
Open your eyes and your mind.

Be a redhead with curls.
Drape long dark hair
over your shoulders.

A wig may be covered
on your insurance
as a hair prosthesis.
Not a bad deal.

Weed your garden

Some stems are not as strong as yours.
Some leaves wither in light frost.

Some folks may be put off
by your parched soil
or your wilted petals.

They are the malady.
They are the plague.
They taint the air.
They stunt your growth.

*Rip them out by their roots
and compost them.*

Don't let weeds
obscure
the beauty of
your bouquet.

Peony, *bashfulness*

Drape yourself with scarves

If your neck will be fat,
    if chins will abound,
if your body will expand,
    accessorize!

Accent your tiny wrists.
Draw attention with splashes of color.

Draw the eye away from girth
with length
    and movement
      and glitter.

Be a petal
or a bud.
Be a rose
or a leaf.

Hibiscus, *delicate beauty*

"John Hopper" Rose, *encouragement*

If life weren't a challenge,
it would be a bore

Nobody promised
life would be
easy.

Nobody promised
life would be
fair.

Meet the challenge
head on.
Go for the gold.
Up close and personally.

This may be
the
triumph
of your life.

Two

Coping with a Chronic Condition

Iris, *message*

Each day that you can do what you want to do is a gift

Be thankful.

Get a pedicure.
Spray a house plant.
Reread a Robert Frost poem.

Forget about what you can't do.

Concentrate on
the best
today
has in store.

Sweet Pea, *delicate pleasures*

Day Lily, *coquetry*

Go easy on yourself

You only pass through here once.

Pick a wild flower.
Have a coffee banana milkshake.
Skip aerobics.

Seize the moment!

Christmas Rose, *"Relieve my anxiety"*

Talk to someone

Whether it's your husband,
an old boyfriend,
your best friend,
a psychologist, or
a cleric,
choose one
person you can talk to.

Or perhaps two.

Tell them your knee hurts.
Tell them your nails are splitting.
Tell them you feel like
a painful ball
is bouncing in your throat.

Talking is like soup.
It's good for what ails you.

Know when to listen

Even the person
you choose
to talk to
has a saturation point.
Try not to water-log
your listener.

You need to express your concerns.
Then think about your confidante.

And ask about
the job situation
or the kids
or the parents
or the knitting
or politics
or whatever interests
him or her.

Listen with interest.

White Lily and Sweet Violet, *modesty*

Gardenia, *transport of joy*

Enjoy nature

Feel the breeze.
Smell the gardenias.

The blues and pinks and purples
of the sky and
the greens of the grasses
and the leaves
are the colors
that give us life.

And they're yours.

Put them in your path.
Keep them in your view.

Weep when you can

You are a part of nature.
And part of your nature is awry.

Crying can purge the worst of what you feel.
Crying can let your natural happiness
resurface.

Watch *Casablanca* or
An Affair to Remember.
Read *The Prince of Tides.*

When you start to cry,
let it out.
Cry so you can laugh again.

No matter how bad you were feeling,
you will feel better
when your tears have flowed
and your nose is blown.

Purple Hyacinth, *tears, sorrow*

Crocus, *abuse not*

Listen to your body

Nobody knows your body
better than you do.

Don't ignore good advice,
but
be prepared
to say no.

Only you
know what
you are feeling.

Listen carefully
to all
that's about.

Three

Preparing for Surgery

Flowering Almond, *hope*

There's more to us
than surgeons can remove

No matter what the surgeon will do,
you are still you.

No one touches your psyche.
No one tweaks your soul.

No one can.

They're all yours.

Magnolia, *dignity*

Passion Flower, *faith*

Welcome prayers and good wishes

It's now known for certain.
Prayers have power.
Prayers help heal.

Gather them all together.
Let them make you well.

Conquer your fear

Acknowledge your fears.
Let them out.

Feel them.
Face them.

Then put them to bed.

Let them out again
when you feel you need to.

They are your fears.
You are in control.

Marigold, *grief, despair*

Write down your wishes

Select burial or cremation.

Suggest your philosophy of life.

Bequeath cash to your closest relatives.

Leave your favorite ladle
to the niece
whom no one likes.

Leave your great-grandmother's wedding band
to the oldest in the next generation.

Make a few copies
of these most important words.
Tell the person closest to you
where to find them.

Zinnia, *thoughts of absent friends*

Phlox, *agreement*

Get a second opinion

Doctors don't always agree.
And surgery is significant.

See a second doctor.
Bring your films and records.

His or her opinion
will either bear out the first
or confirm the need for additional information.

If the opinions differ,
have the doctors converse.

Their discussion may end in agreement.
If it doesn't,
you need to understand
why not.

If your doctors won't talk to each other,
find doctors who will.

Choose your surgeon carefully

Look into his or her education,
board certification,
years of experience,
type of experience, and
experience in the surgery you require.

Even professional affiliations and
published works
may be important.

*When you have all the information you need,
choose the best person for the job.*

But make sure this is someone you can talk to,
someone who will talk to you,
someone who will answer your questions,
someone you have confidence in,
someone with a sense of humor.

Hepatica, *confidence*

Oleander, *beware*

Ask lots of questions

Ask about the procedure.
Ask about the surgical team.
Ask who will do what.

Ask about the hospital.
Ask about the floor you'll be on.

Ask about your recuperation.
Ask how long it will take.
Ask what you can expect.
Ask whether you'll need someone
with you at home
—and for how long.

Ask about possible complications.
Ask for patient references.

Listen to the answers.

Talk to your children

If you have children,
sit down with them
and tell them what's going on.

Explain what they should expect.
Talk through any issues they raise.
Answer their questions.

Serve them herbal tea and
ripe strawberries
dipped in honey.

Look them in the eye.
Be honest.

Cinquefoil, *maternal affection*

Pink Geranium, *preference*

Gather your favorite things

Pack your brightest lipstick and
your favorite book of poetry.
Pack your cuticle cream.

Pack a picture book and
a puzzle book.
Pack your journal
and a pen.

Pack lip balm and
emery boards and
a mirror.

Pack a cheap cassette player
and something by Rogers and Hammerstein.

Take your special things with you.
—And don't forget your toothbrush.

Four

Heading to the Hospital

Sweet Basil, good wishes

Gloxinia, *a proud spirit*

You have beauty and strength
that some are fighting
to retain

Floors below you,
someone has just arrived
in the emergency room.

This person is struggling
for life itself.

You're just getting better.

Pamper your nurses

Nurses tend your garden.

Nurses
respond to care
themselves.

Smile at them.
Ask about their children.

Give them the box of chocolates
you didn't want to eat.

Compliment them on their
white teeth.

Caring goes both ways.

Orchid, *thoughts*

Cornflower, *delicacy*

Pamper your taste buds

As soon as you are allowed,
                have someone bring
    your favorite food
        from a nearby restaurant.

    Nothing
        in a hospital
tastes better than
        pastrami on rye or
Thai soft spring rolls or
    spaghetti with white clam sauce.

                    Savor each morsel.

    Chase with fresh raspberries.

Use lots of lip balm

When your lips are moist and sensual,
you feel more like yourself.

Coat your lips with balm.

You'll feel
sexy and
silky and
soft as a petal.

Dried Flax, *utility*

Sunflower, *haughtiness*

Put some light on the subject

All living things need light.

You are no exception.

When the nurse
tucks you into bed,
she will hand you the light switch.

If she doesn't,
ask for it.

Light is a good thing.

So is darkness
when you want it.

Water your garden

Make sure you have
a good supply of water
and crushed ice.

Drink your fill.

Water is good food.

Cactus Flower, *warmth*

Garden Anemone, *forsaken*

Make sure you
have your glasses

Flowers and people
respond to light
and color
and form.

If you wear glasses or contact lenses,
make sure
they are within reach

Being able to see gives you more control.

You will want to see the flowers and your visitors.

Morning Glory, *affection*

Wear silk pajamas when your mother comes to visit

Or your paisley night gown.
And your bunny slippers.

Drape your flowered robe across the bed.

Allow your mother to become part of the landscape.

Five

Recuperating

Chinese Chrysanthemum,
cheerfulness under adversity

Take it slow and easy

You've been through a bunch.

Bide your time.
Pamper yourself.

Reread *Little Women.*
Watch *Great Chefs of the West.*

Sprinkle baby powder in your slippers.

*You'll be up and around
before you know it.*

You'll be adding Cheer to a light load
soon enough.

For now,
rest on a bed of clover.

White Poppy, *sleep*

Dahlia, *instability*

Healing is an
up-and-down process

You're on a see-saw.

Don't get discouraged
when progress is slow.

You'll be on the upside
looking over the horizon
in good time.

Look at the sky
and breathe
deeply.

Try to enjoy the ride.

Your hair gets a little longer every day

Even Yul Brynner fans
want hair.

Hair you will have.

Wear a turban.
Wrap a scarf.
Tilt your hat brim.
Fuss with your wig.

Underneath,
your hair is growing.

When you have something to work with,
make an appointment
with your beautician.

Balsam, *impatience*

It's okay to be a little crazy

Imagine your fist sailing through a wall.

Scream at the ceiling.

Change your PJs
every hour.

If you don't feel like seeing people,
tell them not to visit.

This is your time.

Use it
to make you
whole
again.

Wallflower, *fidelity in adversity*

Blue Salvia, *"I think of you"*

Take care of someone else

Even when you can't take care of everything,
there are little things you can do.

Write a poem
for the person taking care of you.

Draw a silly portrait
of your very best friend.

Send flowers
to your favorite nurse.

You'll feel better.
So will the person
you do for.

Hug your pet

Stroke his warm fur.
Look into his doey eyes.

Feel the unconditional love.
Feel the strength.
Feel the warmth.

Keep stroking.
Feel the luxury.

Dogwood Blossom, *durability*

Larkspur, *levity, lightheartedness*

Laughter is good medicine

We live in a funny kind of a world.
There's always something to laugh about.

Rent a Billy Crystal movie or
one by the Marx brothers.

Enjoy a
Ziggy or
Peanuts
cartoon book.

Call a funny friend.
Think of something silly.

Laugh, laugh, and laugh some more.

Laughter will heal you.

Variegated Tulip, *beautiful eyes*

Pamper your face

Your beauty is still there.

Put on some makeup,
maybe a little more than you're used to.

Use a bit of concealer.
Try some shadow
under your brow.

Experiment with plum liner
or cherry lipstick
or strawberry blush.

Be creative.
Dare to be outrageous.

Put your best face forward
and wrap it with a smile.

Take a steamy bubble bath

Lollygag in the bathtub.

*Luxuriate in burgundy bubbles
or farkleberry foam.*

Add hot water in slow, thin streams.

Catch up on *InStyle* or *Better Homes & Gardens*.

Watch your fingertips wrinkle.

Damask Rose, *beautiful complexion*

Oriental Poppy, *silence*

Unless you're in a concert hall, avoid giving an organ recital

Telling everyone
all the details of your condition
is boring
(for them)
and endlessly repetitive
(for you).

When someone asks
how you feel,
tell them briefly.

Then change the subject.

*Only doctors
are really interested
in medicine.*

Friends are more interested in flowers.

Review your hospital bill
line by line

Hospitals give good care.
But their billing systems are not infallible.

Go over your invoice
when you feel up to it.

If they charged you for eight aspirin
and you took only six,
call customer service.

Question the hours
you used the oximeter.
What's an oximeter
anyway?

If bone wax
sounds unreasonable,
ask about it.

It's amazing how thrifty you can be.

Pasque Flower, *"You have no claims"*

Get over it!

This is an attitude,
not a command.

*Life is to be lived
and loved
and savored.*

As soon as you can,
get back to the business of living.

Go slowly at first
if you must.

Then give it everything you've got.

Lily of the Valley, *return of happiness*

Six

Returning to Your Normal Routine

Primrose, *early youth*

Re-create yourself

Life has dealt you a slightly different
form or
content.

Look toward the light.
Look into it and make it your own.

Let go of what
you no longer have.

Enhance the rest.

Exploit the best of what's left.

We all want to meet
the new you.

China Rose, *beauty always new*

Clematis, *"I love your mind"*

As soon as you can,
get back to work

If you work
    outside the home,
go back to the office.
    You may want to start
      with a few hours a day.

      If you work at home,
        start gradually.
     But once you start,
      do a little more
        every day.

Beginning your daily activities again
will make you feel
more like the you
that you cherish.

Sweet William, *gallantry*

Do something for someone else

Make a difference.

Teach an adult to read.
Sponsor a child in Burundi.
Donate to the Red Cross.

It doesn't have to be anything major.
Give your old clothes and books to charity.
Volunteer an hour a week.
Help to change a life.

If you can't,
give someone you love
a puffy white cloud.
Or a grand tree.
Or a toothy smile.

A smile is like one open blossom
facing another.

Share what you've learned

Now that you're an expert on
what's happened to you,
    share what you know.

Tell a friend
    or a friend of a friend
who's facing the same thing.

Address a women's group.

Wear a trumpet flower
in your lapel.

Write an article
    for the local paper.

*Nothing feels better
than sharing.*

Hydrangea, *boast*

Purple Columbine, *resolution*

Be well

Feel well and
    stay well.

    And when anyone asks
      how you are,
        answer,
  "Terrific" or
"Fantastic" or
  "Fantabulous."
        Or
  just plain "Well, really well."
  And smile
  and thank them for asking.

*Your life will blossom
in rich color
and full light.*

Editor's Note

THE ASSOCIATION OF FLOWERS WITH MEANING has existed as a literary genre for centuries. Floral vocabulary used in *Watering Wilted Flowers* has its roots in seventeenth-century European society, when the French marquis de Montausier commissioned a gift of illustrated floral poetry, *La guirlande de Julie*, for his fiancée. Fashionable variations on the theme followed, appearing in gift books and almanacs for the gentility. In 1819, publication of Charlotte de Latour's *Le langage des fleurs* popularized the concept of a floral language, which spread to England during the 1820s. Since then, authors both in England and in the United States have written many volumes defining and discussing the intriguing language of flowers. For more information, see *The Language of Flowers: A History* by Beverly Seaton. Published by University Press of Virginia, 1995.

Chamomile, *energy in adversity*